Joe Cone

Heart and Home Ballads

A book of New England verse

Joe Cone

Heart and Home Ballads
A book of New England verse

ISBN/EAN: 9783744789066

Printed in Europe, USA, Canada, Australia, Japan

Cover: Foto ©Thomas Meinert / pixelio.de

More available books at **www.hansebooks.com**

HEART

AND

HOME BALLADS

A BOOK OF NEW ENGLAND VERSE

BY

JOE CONE

ILLUSTRATED.

NEW ENGLAND

New England first, New England last, New England all the time ; New England bound in stately prose, New England clad in rhyme ; New England quaint, New England rare, New England proud and free, New England for the rich and poor, New England e'er for me * * * New England honored far and wide, New England staunch and true ; New England fought for God and right, as she will always do. New England, freedom, liberty, historical and grand, New England, cradle of the just, the well-spring of our land * * * New England first, New England last, New England all the time, New England clad in graceful prose, New England sung in rhyme ; New England quaint, New England rare, New England fair to see, New England once, New England twice, New England three times three!

PRESS OF
L. E. SMART
CAMBRIDGE, MASS.
1899

TO THE FEW

The author has no apologies to offer as they wouldn't be understood, any more than will the poems he now collects for the first time.

To my father and mother, New Englanders staunch and true, who have done so much for me and for whom I can do so little, I lovingly dedicate this, my first book.

[Many of the poems in this volume are used through the courtesy of *The National Magazine, The Boston Courier, Puck, Truth, The New York Herald, The Sunday World, The Detroit Free Press, and The Dramatic News.* The poems, "Two Boys," "Mary Ann," "Sinking The Merrimac," "The Battleship Oregon," "Pick'relin' On Lizzard Crick," and "Popperty's Girl," were written for this volume and have never before appeared in print.]

You take the crowded city streets,
  With life and shops galore :
I'll take the little woodland paths
  Down by the river shore.
You take the public gardens where
  All is arranged by plan :
I'll take the scenes laid out by God,
  And undisturbed by man.

You take the fountain on the lawn,
  And listen to its tale :
I'll listen to the little brook
  That murmurs through the vale.
You live the artificial life,
  And I will live the real :
And joy will come to me in mine
  That yours can ne'er reveal.

CONTENTS

CHILDHOOD POEMS.

WAR POEMS.

".. Upon the sunny Western slope, my boyhood homestead stands."

JIM COULTER'S VIOLIN.

I.

Jim Coulter was a farmer's boy of fifteen summers
    just.

His form was clad in "older clothes," his face and
    feet in dust.

But Jim was smarter than he looked, and music was
    his bread.

"Could play a tune on anything," so all the neigh-
    bors said,

"An' stid uv hangin' round the stores or larkin' with
    the rest,

Wus allus makin' instruments fur which he seemed
    persest."

But Jim had trouble from a source you scarce would
    ever guess ;

His father laughed and poohed and scoffed at all such
    foolishness ;

And presently became so harsh that Jim was forced
    to steal

Away each time he wished to work or play a jig or
    reel.

"This farm work must be carried on," Jim's father
    said one day,

"An' any traps o' your'n I find I'll smash without
    delay !"

Jim had no tender comforter,—she slumbered 'neath
    the hill ;
And so he delved upon the farm with saddened face
    and still.
But boyish dreams and boyish hopes could not be
    driven in ;
Jim stole away on rainy days and made a violin.
" A crude affair?" why to be sure, but marvelous
    for Jim,
And brought to light the hundreth time that genius
    lurked in him.
And Jim was justly proud of it and kept it hid
    away,
But Farmer Coulter's search for eggs unearthed it
    'neath the hay.

He fumed and raved and raised it high to dash upon
    the floor,
Then dropped his arm in partial shame and looked it
    o'er and o'er.
" No, no," said he, " I can't do that, but he will
    never see
This cussed piece uv foolishness, not while he lives
    with me."

Not many hours went by before Jim found his treasure
    gone ;
He threw himself upon the hay too tearful and
    forlorn.
Then slowly rising, full of wrath, his soul ablaze
    within,
Demanded of the cruel man his little violin.

" Yewr violin, yew lazy scamp?" the angry farmer
    cried ;
" Yew might as well ask me fur wealth an all the
    world beside."
" Then," cried the boy with flashing eye, his form
    drawn tall and thin,
" You'll never see my face again till I've that violin!"

      *   *   *   *

II.

Ten years went by but not a word
From Jim had Farmer Coulter heard.
At first he cursed the vagrant Jim,
And had as soon be rid of him.

But as old age o'ertook the man
He lost contentment in his plan,
And on the kitchen wall he hung
The little violin unstrung,

In hopes that Jim some day might call
And guess its mission on the wall.
But he came not ; another year
Went by and he began to fear

That Jim would never come again ;
And broader, deeper, grew his pain.
Long lines of care marked deep his brow,
His hair and beard were snow white now.

While strolling o'er the hill one day
He saw a Boston paper lay,
In careless folds upon the grass,
Where mountain tourists often pass.

And glancing o'er this caught his eye :—
" In Music Hall, assisted by
" James Coulter's famous western band,
" A mammoth, summer concert, grand ! "

*   *   *   *   *   *

III.

An anxious crowd pressed round the door
    Of Music Hall that night ;
Without, was naught but push and roar,
    Within, was gay and light.

The famous band was on the stage,
    Conductor Coulter bowed ;
And then a man infirm with age
    Sobbed " Jim, oh ! Jim," aloud.

For there he stood his long-lost boy,
    So grand and proud and tall ;
Conducting that big orchestra
    In Boston Music Hall.

The clashing strains rose wild and strong,
    Then echoed strangely sweet ;
And Farmer Coulter borne along,
    Grasped firmly to his seat.

He could not understand the spell,
  Nor where 'twas taking him;
And little cared, the truth to tell,
  For was he not with Jim?

When all was o'er, the music hushed,
  And Home Sweet Home was sung,
The farmer to the platform rushed,
  And to a parcel clung.

And with a glow upon his face
  Like one released from sin,
He sobbed aloud with his embrace :—
  " Here—Jim's—yewr violin ! "

BY AND BY.

By an by I'll git my pole,
       By an by.
There'll be heaven in my soul,
       By an by.
I will steal away frum ma
Down to where the fishes are ;
I will spit upon my hook,
An I'll drop it in the brook,
       By an by.

Ma will miss me frum the yard
       By an by.
She will holler for me hard,
       By an by.
But the gurgle uv the stream
Like enough will drown her scream ;
An I'll fish an fish away
Where the speckled beauties lay,
       By an by.

If I ketch a likely mess
       By an by.
Ma will smile with happerness
       By an by.

But —
If I hev an empty creel
Somehow I kin sorter feel
How that apple sprout will dance
On the seat uv my ol pants,
By an by !

DRIVING HOME THE COWS.

Along the shady country road at silent eventide,
  Which wound half choked by running vines and
    overhanging boughs,
Down to the distant pasture, oft we loitered side
  by side,
  Sweet Jessie Doane, we two alone, behind the lazy
    cows.

'Twas sweet that hour at eventide, 'twas sweet to be
  with her,
  And tender were those thoughts of mine her pres-
    ence did arouse ;
And I loved her, yes, I loved her, with a passion all
  astir,
  For she was fair, and none were there, while driv-
    ing home the cows.

And so we trod the country road each fading summer
  day,
  And through the autumn when the frost had
    painted red the boughs ;
And still I feared to tell her what my heart bade me
  to say,
  For fear she might not come again, to stroll behind
    the cows.

15

But as the heart commands the tongue, ere long I
 spake the word,
And sweetly did she turn to me with lovelight
 'neath her brows,
And say that she would have me,—sweetest tones I
 ever heard ! —
Providing she each night with me could stroll
 behind the cows.

JUST THE SAME TO-DAY.

I.

Just the same are things to-day
As in days long passed away,
I can hear those sounds I cherish when I pause to
list awhile ;
Just the same are sweet birds singing,
Just the same soft cow-bells ringing,
Rhyming, swinging,
Chiming, singing,
As when I used to wander to the river through the
stile.

Refrain :

Just the same can I hear,
Boyhood sounds all so dear,
If I pause awhile to listen to their charm ;
And once more I seem to be
Just a blithsome boy so free,
A-roaming through the wildwood on the farm.

II.

Just the same the river flows
Where the wild carnation grows,
I can see its winding azure when I close my eyes to
dream ;

Just the same are lillies growing,
Just the same soft breezes blowing,
  Swaying, flowing,
  Playing, blowing,
As when I gathered mosses from the bank beside the
  stream.

Refrain :

Just the same can I hear
Boyhood sounds all so dear,
If I pause awhile to listen to their charm ;
  And once more I seem to be
  Just a blithsome boy so free,
A-roaming through the wildwood on the farm.

BOYHOOD DAYS.

O take me back to the boyhood days,
  To my boyhood's happy dreaming;
To the leaf-clad hills and the rhythmic rills
  Where the sun-kissed stream lay gleaming.
O take me back to the golden days,
  To the simple joys I tasted ;
For an older life in this toil and strife
  Is a life grown cold and wasted.

I've tasted the fruits of middle age,
  I have found them tart and bitter ;
I have found that fame and a lauded name
  Is only a passing glitter.
So take me back to the boyhood time,
  Where the great ghost life is hidden ;
And lose me there in the woodland fair
  Where grief and care are forbidden.

TWO BOYS.

Sile Grover lived in Gungawamp an farmed it more
    or less :
Fur forty year he'd tilled the soil with more or less
    success.
He lived a quiet, humly life, an allus paid his bills,
An took no int'rist in affairs beyend his stretch uv
    hills.
He labored hard an labored long, an dug a livin
    out,
An met the stormy days uv life with honest heart an
    stout,
No burnin flame harrassed his soul, ambitions none
    had he,
He lived the highest type uv life, rare, sweet sim-
    plicity.
He went tur church an Sunday school, an hed a class
    uv boys,
An counted keepin well the days ermong his simple
    joys.
An when he some tur die his end wuz peaceful ez
    could be,
His work wuz done, his life well spent, frum sin an
    sorrer free.

He lived the highest type uv life, the great an holy
    plan,
An when he died he died at peace with God, himself
    an man.

     *   *   *   *   *   *

Tom Jason left his father's farm at sixteen years uv
    age
Tur dash his name with boyish haste ercrost the
    city's page.
The country was too slow fur him, an tho' he
    worshipped Sile,
He couldn't stay in Gungawamp, it hed no dash an
    style.
He found a place an went tur work, an rose ez bright
    boys do,
An j'ined the firm at twenty-one, a hustler through
    an through.
No scheme wuz big enough fur him tur handle any-
    time,
No hour wuz late enough tur work ef he could gain
    a dime ;
No sum wuz big enough tur save, an so each year
    tur come
He tried with all his might an main tur double every
    sum.
Ambitious, full uv youthful fire, he entered poller-
    tics,
An snatched a moment now an then fur clubs an
    social cliques.

A busy man Tom Jason wuz, "a hustler through an
    through,"
Furever strivin after gain, furever in a stew ;
An tho he wuz successful, ez the world looks on
    success,
At thirty year his health broke down frum overwork
    an stress.
Deprived uv his great hope in life he sank in rapid
    pace,
An died a-cryin out fur gold tur save him frum dis-
    grace.

   *   *   *   *   *   *

Two stuns p'int straight at heaven's blue in Gunga-
    wamp's church yard ;
One over in the corner an one on the boolevard.
One is a stylish monument, a grandlike thing tur see,
An one a modest three-foot slab without no fillergree.
One is Tom Jason's monument, an one Sile Grover's
    stun,
Two boys, clus frens fur sixteen year, whose lives so
    diffrunt run ;
One representin dash an style an stress an worriment,
The other, peace an good ol age, an humble life
    content.

MY YELLER LEGGED RUSTER.

I hed a little ruster once,
　A cur'us little feller ;
His tail warn't growed, nur wuz his spurs,
　But both his laigs wuz yeller.
He'd tag me all eroun the farm,
　Could fight, an allus win it ;
Could lick a ruster twice ez small
　In less'n ha'f a minute.

'At ruster?　He knowed ever'thing,
　You couldn fool him, nuther ;
Would scoot frum sight when pa come roun
　But warn't afeerd o' mother.
An I, I planned a big career
　Fur 'at air perky chicken,
An hed 'im roun the house so much
　'At I come nigh a lickin.

But one thing he wuz backards in,
　An 'at wuz on his crowin ;
He *wouldn't* crow, an air he wuz
　Purt big an still a-growin.

An I, I cried, an pa, says he,
  " Yew little tow-head shuster,
'At ruster yewrn is er hen,
  An ain't no kind er ruster! "

SALMON RIVER. *

Per'aps yew never heerd uv it, thet silvery stream
uv mine,
Which blinks all day in a drowsy way, where lillies
bloom an shine.
It *ain't* in all the joggerfrys, it's some too small I
s'pose,
It's way down in Connecticut, where wooden nutmegs
grows.

It wiggles frum ermongst the hills fur up beyend the
town,
Then laughs an groans o'er stumps an stones, an
rushes madly down
Tell by an by it stretches out to meet the ebb an
flow,
Then marches back an forards like them reglar
soldiers go.

Upon the sunny western slope my boyhood home-
stid stands,
A tangled mess uv loveliness the toil uv lovin hands ;
An frum the summit uv the hill is spread before my
eyes
A gorgeous spectacle uv land an water parrerdise.

28

I know jest where the fishes live, an where the lillies
    grow.
An where the birds talk lovin words, an where the
    mushrats go :
I know where sets the eagle an the hawk an fisher-
    king,
An where tur find new wintergreen, an where the
    wild grapes swing.

An on the moss-grown bank I set an watch the
    mirrored skies,
Each great white boat in cloudland float beneath my
    raptured eyes.
Ah ! Shakespeare never loved *his* stream no bettern
    I love mine,
Which blinks all day in a drowsy way where lillies
    bloom an shine.

MY DADDY'S VIOLIN.

When daddy face to face did lay
    With that grim monster, death :
He called me to him and did say
    With his departing breath,

" Now, Zeke, I'm goin tur leave ye soon.
    (Sho, sho, now don't begin)
An promise me tur keep in tune
    Y'r daddy's vierlin.

" I kennot take it over there,
    Tho' oft I wish I might ;
So I mus leave it in *your* care,
    Now promise, Zeke, tur-night.

" It's cheered my heart fur many years,
    It's kep me frum despair ;
It's kep away the doubts an fears
    Uv a life full uv care.

'An Zeke, wen storms uv life rip things,
    Yew take the vierlin
An draw the bow acrost the strings,
    An let y'r heart jine in.

" But when I'm gone—there there, my boy—
    Jes lay it on my breast ;
An leave it there in silent joy
    Tell I am laid tur rest :

" *Then take it, use it, make it sing,*
  'Twill keep ye out uv sin!' "
Then he fell back, and every string
  Snapped on that violin.

*   *   *   *   *

'Twas years ago that daddy died—
  How quickly they have sped !
And oftentimes when sore and tried
  I have been comforted

As daddy said I would ; and too,
  I have been kept from sin
By staying in the long nights through
  To play his violin.

DAD'S BIG MELON PATCH.

There wuz a time, in early spring, I dreaded most
    to scratch
From early morn till late at night in dad's big melon
    patch.
The patch it looked ten acres long by seven acres
    wide,
An every hill a mountain top, with valleys close
    beside.

An then the hoe I hed to use weighed all uv twenty
    pound,
An strained the sockets uv my arms at every stroke
    an bound ;
The soil, tho' light, it seemed to hug the dusty earth
    like lead,
An every hill I hed to make choked up my soul with
    dread.

An every year in early spring I dreaded most to
    scratch
With heavy hoe an achin hand in dad's big melon
    patch.
Yew see the river lay close by, an sparkled in the
    sun,
Jes tantalizin uv my soul with every gleam it spun ;

An every ripple, all day long, jes beckoned me
 aside,
An showed me where a fish lay hid beneath the silver
 tide.
An wen all this wuz hauntin me, how could a feller
 scratch
With stiddy stroke an right good will in dad's ol
 melon patch?

But wen the autumn sun shone warm, an dew lay
 on the grass,
An we hed shocked the field uv corn, an housed the
 garden sass,
An wen the nuts begun to turn, an cockle burrs to
 catch,
I hed no dread to spend an hour in dad's big melon
 patch!

Fur there would glisten in the sun them fellers, long
 an green,
With meller, juicy, red insides, fit fur a king or
 queen;
An w'en a-straddle uv the fence, with melons a hull
 batch,
I soon furgot my sufferin's in dad's big melon patch.

An so it is with every soul, the hull great human
 batch,
We hev our mole-hill mountains here in life's big
 melon patch;
We murmur an we magnify, an dread to do a job,
An look out on the river, yearnin fur its lazy throb.

We fain would throw away the hoe an laze beside
        the stream.
An let the melons plant themselves, an fish an idly
        dream.
But wen at last success hez come we gobble down
        our catch.
An soon furgit the trials we've hed in life's big melon
        patch.

" Yew see the river lay close by an sparkled in the sun."

EUGENE FIELD.

The little folks' friend has passed away,
  And his pen is covered with rust ;
For the Lord is good, and he takes his own
  For a higher and nobler trust.
" O, the years are many, the years are long,"
  And our hearts are tried and sore ;
But we wait, Eugene, till the last great scene,
  To listen and laugh once more.

The trumpet and drum shall beat and call,
  Though their champion's voice is stilled ;
And Wynken and Blynken asleep shall fall,
  Of thy fancies their visions filled.
" O, the years are many, the years are long,"
  But in the far-off days to be,
Thy sweet, sweet rhymes of the childhood times
  Shall be sung at the mother's knee.

And little Boy Blue shall lisp thy name,
  In his mother's arms at eve :
And she shall tell of the poet king,
  And thy mystic tales shall weave.
" O, the years are many, the years are long,"
  We fain would learn what they screen ;
But we know thy songs shall delight the throngs
  Forever and ever, Eugene.

KEEP ON A-FISHIN'.

Suppose the fish don't bite at fust,
　　What be yew goin tur dew?
Chuck down yewr pole, throw out yewr bait,
　　An say yewr fishin threw?
Uv course yew hain't, yewr goin tur fish
　　An fish an fish an wait
Until yew've ketched yewr basket full,
　　An used up all yewr bait.

Suppose success don't come at fust,
　　What be yew goin tur dew?
Throw up the sponge, an kick yewrself,
　　An go tur feelin blew?
Uv course yew hain't, yewr goin tur fish,
　　An bait an bait ergin;
Bimeby success will bite yewr hook,
　　An yew will pull him in.

EVERY DAY.

Life is growin brighter,
   Every day ;
Souls are growin whiter
   Every day.
Birds are singin sweeter,
Girls are lookin neater,
Life it grows completer
   Every day.

What's the use uv sighin
   Any day ?
What's the use uv cryin
   Any day ?
Wear an tear is killin,
Sorrer is tew willin,
Don't good tears be spillin
   Any day.

Keep yewr song a-goin
   Every day ;
Keep yewr music flowin
   Every day.
Cast off sad repinin,
Shine the murky linin,
Keep the sun a-shinin
   Every day.

A DREAM OF LIZZARD CRICK.

Turnight my heart is longin an my pulse is beatin
    quick,
Cuz my thoughts hev gone a-driftin to the banks uv
    Lizzard Crick ;
To the scenes uv child an boyhood, to the stream I
    wooed an won,
Where the lillies on its bosom nod an sparkle in the
    sun.
An I see the grasses wavin an I hear a little " swish,"
An I know it is a mushrat or a greedy, startled fish,
An I reach my hand beside me, then I draw it back-
    ward quick
When I find I *ain't* a-fishin on the banks uv Lizzard
    Crick.

I kin see the darkened eddies where the water circles
    roun,
Bearin chips an foamy white-cups, ever ridin up an
    down ;
I kin see the slantin shadders ez they play ercrost
    the stream,
An the winders threw the branches castin here an
    thire a gleam.

I kin see the sandy bottom where the smaller stream
    unites,
Ever creepin further, further, ez each grain uv sand
    alights,
An I laugh ez I remember how our toes would never
    stick
To the bottom ez we youngsters tried tur wade ercrost
    the crick !

Frum the bend above the footbridge I kin hear a
    boy's " halloo,"
An I know thet Bill Buzzey is a-comin crickward
    too ;

An I answer with a warwhoop thet goes ringin down
      the glen,
An in less'n haf a minute we are "strippin off"
      ergen!

*   *   *   *   *   *

O the river's way off yender, miles an miles beyend
      my gaze ;
Years hev come an years hev wandered since them
      keerless, happy days ;
But thank God my dreams lie closer, an they crowd
      my vision thick,
While my heart beats warm ez ever fur the banks uv
      Lizzard Crick.

DOWN ON THE MILL STREAM.

Some rave about the Pallersades
   Down on the Hudson river ;
An some about Niagara falls
   Thet make a feller shiver.
An some will long tur see the land
   Where Shakespeare lived an writed.
An some the city uv Paree
   Thet's allus gay an lighted.
But ez fur me, jest humly me,
   Fur years I've sorter wished
Thet I could see the ol mill stream
   Where long ago I fished.

An folks will go in exterey
   About the land uv flowers,
An on the field uv Gettysburg
   Waste many precious hours ;
Then come along tur Washington
   (I kinder hate tur pen it)
An heng around tur shake the hand
   Uv president an senate.
But ez fur me, jest humly me,
   'Twould make me fairly scream
Tur shake ergen the hand uv Ben
   Down by the ol mill stream.

41

DOWN ON THE MILL STREAM

An I would give my hull estate
    Once more tur go in swimmin
Off frum the rocks at allus wuz
    Shunned by the gals an wimmin.
Ah yes, them places uv repute
    No doubt hev many pleasures;
Them moozeums an battle grounds
    Uv antick relic treasures.
But ez fur me, jest humly me,
    I hev but one life dream;
An thet's tur spen a week with Ben
    Down on the ol mill stream.

LABOR TO CAPITAL.

My heart is sick and my soul is sick
 Of the shameful greed of men ;
Of the endless crush and the headlong rush
 That stifles this world of ken.
O, the heedless strife and the needless strife
 Which blackens the skies that be :
It is all for gain that we suffer pain,
 And it cripples both you and me.

I'm sick of the rich man's avarice,
 Of his daily poorhouse dread ;
I'm sick of the strife that haunts the life
 Of the soul who toils for bread.
The poor man's snarl and the rich man's sneer
 Go ringing from sea to sea :
And the discord jars from the earth to stars,
 And it rankles both you and me.

I'm sick of the sight and sound of trade,
 'Tis nothing but Godless schemes :
And the fool who dreams of his honest schemes
 Is a dreamer of Godless dreams.
But there is a way, if we only would,
 To lighten the burdens that be :
To sweeten the life and kill this strife,
 And it rests with both you and me.

BILLY BUZZEY.

Yew all know Billy Buzzey cuz yew see him every-
  where,
Jest look out on the corner an yew're sure tur find
  him there ;
Look up or down the river, or in any hidin place
An yew'll find Billy Buzzey there with freckles on
  his face.
They ain't a blessed thing in town at Billy doesn
  know,
They ain't a blessed danger place at Billy wouldn
  go :
Fact Billy he's a wonder, jest a bottom dollar brick,
The same ez my ol Billy on the banks uv Lizzard
  Crick.

  Billy Buzzey, Billy Buzzey,
    I am writin this tur yew :
  Billy Buzzey, Billy Buzzey,
    Dear ol Billy tried an true !
  Years may come an years may wander,
    We're apart an older grown :
  But I'll love yew Billy Buzzey,
    Jest ez long ez love is known.

44

O the days with Billy Buzzey, wen so carefully we
    stole
To the bridge behind the sawmill an unwound our
    fishin pole ;
How cautiously we flattened on the warped an twisted
    plank
Tur see ef any shiners wuz a hidin neath the bank.
Billy Buzzey he could ketch em wen no other feller
    could,
He could track a coon or otter threw the thickest uv
    the wood ;
He could climb the highest tree top, he would never
    take a stump,
An they warn't no sech a fighter in the hull uv Gun-
    gawamp !

Billy Buzzey, Billy Buzzey,
    I am writin this tur yew ;
Billy Buzzey, Billy Buzzey,
    Dear ol Billy good an true.
Years may come an years may wander,
    An we kennot stop their flow.
But I'll love yew, Billy Buzzey,
    Long ez love is mine tur know.

SING A SONG.

Sing a song uv Hope, sir,
　Ef yew are bound tur sing :
A million ears are list'nin
　Tur hear its cheery ring.
A song uv praise is precious,
　A song uv truth is blest :
A song uv love is pretty,
　A song uv Hope is *best*.

Sing a song uv Hope, sir,
　An sing it with a zest :
A million souls are weary,
　A-waitin fur its rest.
A song uv praise is welcome,
　Tur foller care an strife :
A song uv joy is restful,
　A song uv Hope is *life*.

THE SUMMER FEELIN.

O I like the summer feelin with its hazy, lazy air,
An its soft an drowsy whisper threw the trees :
I like its meller music which is risin everywhere,
Frum the waterfalls an thrushes an the drone uv
busy bees.

O I like the summer feelin with its drowsy monotone,
Uv toads an bugs an locusts, an the crickets' inter-
lude :
I like tur lie an listen with the branches o'er me
thrown
Where the brooklet meets the river an the medder
meets the wood.

Yes, I like the summer feelin cuz it fills my hungry
soul
With a glow uv healthy happerness thet nuthin else
kin do :
An I look up threw the branches where the great
white cloudlets roll,
An I feel myself a-driftin off tur worlds beyend the
blue.

With the windin Crick beside me, an the restful skies
above,
An a tangled mess uv mosses lyin 'neath me for a
bed :

An a splash uv summer feelin frum the green-clad
   hills I love.
An a strain uv Natur's music runnin wildly threw my
   head.

Do yew know the summer feelin?   If yew don't then
   steal away
Where the medder meets the woodlan an the brook-
   let meets the stream :
Let yewr heart beat tur the music, let yewr loosened
   fancies play,
An loaf an loiter by the Crick, an dream an dream an
   dream.

MY OL' DAD.

There wuz a time once when I had
More common sense en my ol dad,
An yuster tell him what wuz what
Wen he a leetle contry got ;
An wen he tried tur kick up sin
I hed hard work tur hol him in.
The hardes trials them days I had
Wuz in the managemunt uv dad.

But mother warnt so hard tur hol ;
She allus done ez she wuz tol
An never thought uv sayin no,
Wen I tol her, "dew so an so."
She realized jest what I wuz,
Ez wise ol mothers allus does,
An kep herself frum day tur day,
Eccordin tew my better way.

But dad he warnt so bright ez ma,
An we wuz allus in a jar :
Tell one day in the onion bed,
He disobeyed some things I said,
Wich shocked my dignerty, an riled
My sense uv jestice tell she biled.
An so I says, " It's jest erbout
Time now we hed this bizniz out."

Wall, there aint very much tur tell.
Twuz sevral days fore I got well ;
An ma hed tew reseat my pants.
Wen dad hed finished off his dance.
An now, ef I remember right,
I changed my min somewhat thet night ;
An ever sence thet summer's day.
I've let my daddy hev his way.

NOT A CANDIDATE.

I ain't no kind uv cannerdate fur office here this Fall ;
I'm out uv politics an sich, an out fur good an all.
It hain't no use a-coaxin me, I won't put down my
    name ;
I ain't a-hankerin jest now fur town or county fame.
I've hed my full uv politics, I know the hull durn
    thing.
An Gungawamp will hev tur run without me in the
    ring.
A man thet tens tur bizzerniz, an keeps his farmin
    straight,
Ain't got no time fur politics, an I'm no cannerdate.

No, no! tut! tut! Yew unnerstan I've given yew my
    word :
Yew fellers air the mos persistin chaps I ever heard.
Why durn my boots! ef yew heng on I'll be a gettin
    riled,
An wen I git my back up, boys, I aint no peaceful
    child.
I've run fur slectman forty times, an twenty times
    fur clerk,
An every time some fellerd bolt—my ticket wouldn
    work.
I've jest concluded this ere Fall tur shun yewr
    temptin bait ;
I dont want none uv politics an I'm no cannerdate.

O, yaas! yewr promerses er good, yewr argymunts er
    fine ;
I'll "sweep the county " an I'll bring the " doubtful"
    inter line.
A hundred cash will dew it all — yew think I'm purty
    green ;
Yew are the mos persistin chaps thet I hev ever seen.
Now looky here, I tol yew once, I'm gittin purty
    mad ;
Altho ef I *could* sweep the town it wouldn be so bad.
Why durn my boots!   I blieve I kin ; I'll try at any
    rate ;
Bring up some cider, Mary Ann, fur I'm er canner-
    date !

PICK'REL IN WINTER

I know where spreads a silvry stream,
    A stretch uv pure delight ;
Between two lines uv ghostly hills,
    Now frosty, cold an white.
I see long miles uv glistnin snow,
    I hear the forest wail ;
I hear the rumble uv the ice
    Which thunders down the vale.

Mayhap yew think its lonely there,
    An wouldn keer tur go
Where lies a foot or two uv ice,
    An two or more uv snow.
Ef thet is how yew feel, my friend,
    In town so snug an nice,
I guess yew never yit hev pulled
    A pick'rel threw the ice.

MARY ANN.

We lived turgether on the farm, my parents, Dan an
    me,
An we wuz happy an content ez any folks could be ;
Tell mother, bless her weary eyes, who wuzzut over
    stout,
Grew sort o' weak an all run down, an needed helpin
    out,
So wen Bill Smith, the drunkard, died, a wuthless
    sort uv man,
We tuk his little orphan gal whose name wuz Mary
    Ann.
A sweet-faced child ez ever wuz, we loved her, Dan
    an me,
An uster ask her, boyish like, whose gal she wuz tur
    be.

An she would look frum me tur Dan an en frum Dan
    tur me,
Her lustrous eyes a-pleadin like yit full uv witchery,
An say with voice raal low an sweet, (tur still a pet-
    ty fuss,)
At wen she growed up big enough she'd hev the both
    uv us !
The years sped on, yit neither gained the so called
    inside track ;

Wenever Dan drawed her tur school I allus drawed
    her back,
An day by day her face wore signs uv sweet per-
    plexity :
Becuz she didn keer fur Dan no moren she did fur me.
She uster tell us uv a love, a love we never knew,
An said at all would share alike if they wuz good an
    true :
But all the love I keerd about wuz thet uv Mary Ann,
But she, she didn keer fur me no moren she did fur
    Dan.
Then Mary Ann grew beautiful, how beautiful wuz
    she !
Her step, her smile, her evry act wuz grace an purity ;
An each wuz longin fur the time wen he would be a
    man.
An Dan he sorter scowled at me an I scowled back at
    Dan.

Then O, the change at come to us, it's burned into
    my brain,
An all the power uv Heaven an arth kin ne'er remove
    the pain :
Our Mary Ann tuk strangely sick, an one bright
    April day
We laid her yender on the hill then turned our steps
    away.
An wen we come in sight uv home Dan peared tur
    feel so bad
At I, tho shameful ez it wuz, got sorter riled an mad,
An gritted threw my tight shet teeth, with rage an
    jealousy :

" Yew needn feel so tarnal bad, she thought the most
    uv *me*.'"

But Dan he never said one word, an many weeks
    went by,
An en we noticed paler cheeks an dim-like grew his
    eye :
An wen he lay in bed one night I stole up to his side
An ast furgiveness arter which we both shuk hans
    an cried.
An there within thet darkned room I knelt by him tur
    pray,
An ast thet frum my youthful heart all sin be washed
    away ;
An by his bedside on my knees a newer faith began :
The faith which allus seemed a part uv sweet-faced
    Mary Ann.

An wen Dan died one winter's night I sorter wished
    twuz me,
Becuz I knew at he would go beyend the Jasper Sea,
An there would find sweet Mary Ann in angel robes
    uv white,
Who'd welcome him with sunny smiles an ol time
    love an light.
Ah, thet wuz many years ago ; an yit it seems ez clear
Ez tho it wuz but yisterday I saw em standin here.
But wether she wuz his or mine *I*'ve sworn tur be
    a man,
An I would love em were they here, both Dan an
    Mary Ann.

FISHIN' BY AN' BY.

The earth is growin greener,
An the air is gittin cleaner,
They's a sort uv happy twinkle in the dimples uv
    the sky :
Evrybody's steppin lightly,
Evry eye is shinin brightly,
Cuz we're all a-goin fishin by an by.

Down the brook the birds er singin,
On the hills the cow bells ringin,
In the fiel's the plows er cuttin threw the sod so bare
    an dry :
In the house the women's churnin,
At the school the boys er learnin,
An evrybody's happy for the fishin by an by.

Fishin by an by,
With an angle worm an fly :
We are much obleeged tur natur,
She's a bloomin sweet pertater,
Cuz she let's us go a-fishin by an by.

WITH MABEL, NUTTING.

In the golden autumn sunshine,
  With a joyous step and tread,
Do I go with Mabel nutting,
  Where the chestnut branches spread.
Mabel laughs and Mabel frolics,
  Mabel singeth like a dove :
Mabel doesn't fill her basket,
  But she fills my heart with love.

    Nuts are brown and plenty,
      Skies are pure and white ;
    But Mabel is the picture
      That captivates me quite.

Through the woods I stroll with Mabel,
  To the winding homeward lane :
With the promise in my bosom
  That I've tried so long to gain.
Mabel laughs and Mabel frolics,
  Mabel rompeth and is coy :
Mabel hasn't filled her basket,
  But she's filled my heart with joy.

    Nuts are brown and plenty,
      Skies are pure and white ;
    But Mabel is the picture
      That captivates me quite.

58

THE BIMEBY TIME.

Wen the Bimeby Time comes roun this way,
    Wen the Bimeby Time comes roun ;
There'll be less work an lots more play,
    There'll be less hours an lots more pay,
An common men will hev more say,
    Wen the Bimeby Time comes roun.

Wen the Bimeby Time comes roun ;
    O I long tur hear the soun ;
So I'm sittin an a-mopin,
    An a-gropin an a-hopin,
Tell the Bimeby Time comes roun.

Wen the Bimeby Time once gits in view,
    Wen the Bimeby Time gits roun ;
We'll hev free trade an tariff tew,
    Hard times won't trouble me nur yew,
An Sunday'll las the hull week threw,
    Wen the Bimeby Time comes roun.

Wen the Bimeby Time comes roun,
    O I long tur hear the soun ;
So I'm sittin an a-mopin,
    An a-gropin an a hopin,
Tell the Bimeby Time comes roun.

DAD'S OL GRINDSTONE.

Under a spreadin russet bough,
   Uncared for an alone,
Threw summer's sun an winter's snow
   Hez stood dad's ol grindstone.
An I in fancy see it now
   Almos with weeds o'ergrown.

How well I recollect each morn
   Thet dad would call tur me,
At break uv day tur come an turn
   The stone beneath the tree.
An every whirl she 'ud squeak an groan,
   An much exerted be.

My hands would blister, peel an tear,
   But I made ne'er a face :
Twuz better tur be blistered there
   Then on some other place.
So while the lark-songs filled the air
   The grindin went apace.

I steal frum town life oft in ruth
   An look the old scenes threw ;
An though it sounds a bit uncouth
   I find these words come true :
" The work I dreaded so in youth,
   I now would gladly do."

I'm turnin now the stone uv life,
 A-grindin fortune's blade ;
With nicks an cracks extremely rife
 An ruther poorly made.
An oft the stone squeaks in the strife
Like dad's beneath the shade.

SMILES AND TEARS.

I've seen the summer's sun aflame,
 While weeping were the changeful skies ;
I've seen a woman smile the same,
 While pearly tears shone in her eyes.
And both brought visions unto me,
And both were beautiful to see.

THE TIMES THAT USED TO BE.

" I'm always thinkin, thinkin, uv the times that used to
be,
Where the springs and golden autumns flushed the friendly
fields of Lee :
An as I look back yonder, on them fur off plains an
skies,
The sun may be a-shinin, but it's rainin roun my eyes!"

—Frank L. Stanton in "Songs of The Soil."

I, too, am allus thinkin uv the days uv long ago :
I cannot seem to help it sence they crowd my vision so.
A-thinkin, thinkin, thinkin while the golden moments
    flee,
Uv the days uv happy childhood, an the times that
    used to be.
They's people allus thinkin uv the pleasures yet to
    come :
I'll admit anticipation occcypies *my* leisure some,
But furever I'm a-thinkin uv the days that uster be,
Uv the days down in the country where the atmos-
    phere is free.

Uv the singin brooks an medders, broken fences,
    tumbled walls,
Uv the sunshine thro' the branches an the splashin
    waterfalls ;
Uv the cave off in the mountains, playin " Huckle-
    berry Finn,"
An the Injun huts an wigwams, an the battles we
    wuz in.

There wuz " Theerdore's brook " in summer where
    we learned to swim, by jo!
Don't you remember, Arth' an Alvin ?   Bet you can't
    furgit it ; no,
An the sawmill with the kerriage where we uster set
    an ride ;
The mill-pond where the shiners much preferred to
    stay inside !
The raftin thire on Cowdrey's, an the ships we sent
    afloat,
An the argerments presented on who owned the fastes
    boat.
O, life wuz worth the livin but we didn't know it
    then ;
It is only that we see it when we're sad an busy
    men.
But it makes life all the sweeter, an it brings a rest
    to me
To look away off yender on the days that uster be.
O, the days that uster be, boys, thank God fur
    every one !

I wouldn't swap my memories fur all that's 'neath the
       sun.
An you boys in the countryside jest fill your souls
       with it ;
Jest sozzle in the sunshine an preserve it every bit.
Then when you've grown to busy men, you'll hev,
       the same as me,
A golden store uv memories, '' the days that uster be.''

PICKRELIN ON LIZZARD CRICK.

Yew take it in the mornin wen the sun is clouded in,
Wen frum off the water's risin jest a steamy vapor
    thin,
An push yewr boat ermongst the pads where lillies
    nod at yew,
Ats wen the pickrel take a bait an take it spiteful,
    tew.
They aint no fishin equal tew it any place yew go :
A limber pole, a cotton line, a swish, a heave an tow.
Yew jerk yewr bait erlong the aige an purty soon
    yew'll see
A sudden swirl, a silvry gleam, a tuggin enermy,
An then yew pull with all yewr might, with knees an
    elbows stiff,
An out will come a pickerel a-headin fur the skiff.

Ive fished fur many kinds uv fish in brook an lake an
    sea,
But pickrel fishin on the Crick is good enough fur
    me :
They aint no gittin ready, with a lot uv fuss an frills.
They aint no scientific talk erbout the fly thet kills :
They aint no stringin up uv gear, uv patent lines an
    hooks,

An argermunts fur playin game yew read erbout in
      books.
Its jest a throw ermongst the pads, an slop yewr bait
      erlong,
An purty soon yewr line will taut an settle downward
      strong,
An then yew pull with all yewr might, with knees an
      elbows stiff,
An out will shute a pickerel a-headin fur the skiff.

They aint no fishin equal tew it any place yew go:
A long cane pole, a cotton line, a swish, a heave an
      tow.
Its mewsic tur my fishin ear tur hear it swish an
      spat
Upon the surface uv the Crick fust thisaway an that.
I'd ruther stan thire in the boat an swing a limber
      pole
Then be the leader uv a band, I would upon my
      soul !
I'd ruther feel the tuggin uv a pickrel on my line
Then hol a pair uv hosses uv the lates bob design.
Yaas *sir*, give me a pickerel fur good, excitin fun,
An Lizzard Crick fur backgroun an my happerness
      is won !

NATURE'S INSTRUMENT.

The brook which rambles on its way
    And whirls beneath the old brush fence,
Makes music in my ear today,
    As one of Nature's instruments.

I seem to hear it dash along,
    Impatient at the hindering stones;
Then leaping gaily in its song
    Of mingled joy and monotones.

Oft when a boy if aught I had
    A passing sense of worldly pain,
The cadence of that brook-song glad
    Restored my happy self again.

Today, above the irksome round,
    To which this noisy world gives vent,
I hear a sweet, relieving sound,
    The strain of Nature's instrument.

●

CHILDHOOD POEMS

A GOOD-NIGHT SONG.

I.

Mother croons a good-night song,
  Close your eyes my dearie ;
Fairies round a wee one throng,
  Close your eyes my dearie.
Close your eyes while mother sings,
Hear the dip of fairy wings,
Night a peaceful slumber brings,
  Close your eyes my dearie.

> Close your eyes,
>   Little dear ;
> In the skies
>   Stars appear.
> Thro' the light
>   Shadows creep ;
> Dear, good-night,
>   Go to sleep.

II.

Bylo-land in slumber lies,
  Close your eyes my dearie ;
Angels watch you from the skies,
  Close your eyes my dearie.

Slumber while the night wind sighs,
Slumber ere the twilight flies,
Dream of love and lullabies.
  Close your eyes my dearie.

        Close your eyes,
          Little dear ;
        In the skies
          Stars shine clear.
        Fades the light,
          Shadows creep :
        Dear good-night,
          Go to sleep.

POPPERTY'S GIRL.

Popperty's girl has eyes of brown,
  And her cheeks are round and pink ;
Her hair is brown,
        And as soft as down,
  And curly as you can think.
Popperty's girl can talk, ah yes,
  She talks from morning till night ;
And so good is she
        She climbs to my knee
And offers to help me write.
Thus she steals my time day after day,
For popperty never could send her away.

It's popperty this and popperty that,
  And " popperty peet-a-boo ; "
And " popperty *here*,"
        And " popperty *dear*,"
  And " popperty boo-woo-woo ! "

And then I toss her high in the air,
   And give her a gentle whirl :
And she laughs and crows,
         And pulls at my nose,
  For she is popperty's girl !

HER OLD RUBBER DOLL.

The Rubber Doll whistles, the Rubber Doll squeaks,
The Rubber Doll listens and mutters and speaks;
It jumps and it tumbles and oft has a fall,
But nothing can equal her old Rubber Doll.

A hundred times a day our little one kisses it,
A hundred times a day our little one misses it,
   A hundred times a day she makes it squall;
Then she catches it and blesses it,
And smooths it and caresses it,
   And talks very knowing to her old Rubber Doll.

The Rubber Doll scolds and the Rubber Doll squawks,
The Rubber Doll whimpers and grumbles and talks;
It moans and it cries with a pitiful call,
But baby just worships her old Rubber Doll.

A hundred times a day our little one sighs for it,
A hundred times a day our little one cries for it,
   A hundred times a day she lets it fall;
Then she catches it and snugs it up,
And drowsily she hugs it up,
   And drops off to slumber with her old Rubber Doll.

74

A BRAVE LITTLE SOLDIER.

I've just been reading history, about the good old
  days,
About our soldiers fighting, and the Injun's wicked
  ways :
About the British and the Yanks who fought at
  Bunker Hill,
And how the North and South stood ground as only
  soldiers will.

I tell you men were mighty brave and mighty daring
  then,
And I just wish 'at I were big as all the other men :
I'd like to fight 'ith guns and swords, and be a
  soldier too ;
Right in thickest of the fight—hurrah ! now wouldn't
  you ?

What's 'at you say ? I didn't hear ; oh, yes, I did
  forget
To shut the chickens up, mamma, but I will do it yet.
Dear suz, it's dark, my ! what was 'at ? It gave me
  such a fright !
I can't—boo hoo—shut up the h-hens, 'less someone
  holds a light !

THE ACTOR'S CHILD.

The brilliant streets were full of folk,
    All hastening up and down ;
And everywhere was life and light,
    Within the noisy town.
And some were laughing on their way
    And some were silent, sad ;
And some were good and noble folk,
    And some mayhap were bad.

But ever, ever on the move,
    The great throng hurried by ;
Each one upon some mission bent,
    None caring where or why.
But in one lately joyous home,
    Behind dark walls and still ;
Upon a dainty bed of white,
    An actor's child lay ill.

All day the anxious mother watched,
    The hand of death to stay ;
The father, but one hour before,
    Rushed from the matinee.
And now the clock had spoken six,
    The doctor shook his head ;
" An hour, or two, not more than four,"
    And that was all he said.

THE ACTOR'S CHILD

Seven drew near, the actor's brain,
    It seemed, would drive him wild :
He knew his mighty call to go,
    But could not leave his child.
The parents' hands were clasped in love,
    But neither moved nor spoke ;
And when the timepiece chimed again,
    The little one awoke.

She half arose and looked around —
    A heavenly face had she :
And something seemed to whisper that
    She neared eternity.
" Papa," she said, " it's seven o'clock,
    I counted every chime ;
It's very late, why don't you go ?
    You won't—be—there—in—time."

" My child I cannot go to-night,
    My little one is ill ;
I could not leave you, dearest girl.
    Now keep you very still."
" Not go to-night? O, dear papa,
    You shan't stay here with me ;
You must go out, and make them laugh,
    Why—don't—why can't—you—see,

" The people would feel awful bad,
    Christmas would be so dear ;
What would so many people do
    Without *you*, papa dear ?

Now go; please go; my God is good,
　　He doesn't need you here;
He's telling me to have you go,
　　Please—go—now, papa—dear."

One moment more 'twould be too late,
　　The darling slept once more;
The actor, true to art and love,
　　In sorrow paced the floor.
"O, God!" he cried, in silent plea,
　　"Give unto me thine ear;
Where lies my duty, guiding one,
　　O, be it there, or here!"

The loving wife stole to his side,
　　And, pointing, he knew where,
She whispered, like a guiding voice,
　　"Your duty lieth there.
Go; go my husband, do her will,
　　She's in our Father's care;"
And almost reeling to her side,
　　He kissed the golden hair.

"O, God! forgive me, should she die,
　　And I be far away;"
And out he rushed, a burdened man,
　　To play the light and gay.
And folk were pleased with him that night,
　　"A brilliant star," they said;
But every call stabbed deep his heart,
　　And none knew how it bled.

The curtain fell, in costume bold,
　He ran into the street.
And hailed a cabman, whom he knew,
　And home was driven fleet.
And when he saw the mother's face,
　He knew his flower was dead :
" But God was good," the mother smiled,
　" She woke no more," she said.

●

WAR POEMS

1898—1899.

SINKING THE MERRIMAC.

(Santiago Harbor June 3, 1898.)

Into the night she steamed away,
   While an awful silence fell :
Straight for the monsters dark and grim,
   Glutted with shot and shell.

Sombre and swift and silent,
   Scarcely a whispered breath :
On, on towards Santiago,
   On to success or—death.

Grim headlands rose in the distance,
   Old Morro guarding the bay :
Waiting with limbered Hontorias,
   Waiting for a hated prey.

They sleep ! Then apast the entrance
   Leaving a tell-tale track,
Into the sharp curved channel
   Swept the bold Merrimac.

" What's that ? The enemy's picket ?
    A launch—they see us—'tis bad !
A shot—three pounder—they're fighting,
    God, is the tiny thing mad ? "

Then a light flashed over the darkness,
    The enemy sprang to their arms :
The fleet and the forts awakened,
    The night was rent with alarms.

They tried to swing her crosswise,
    Her helm she would not obey :
For the nosing, pursuing picket
    Had shot her rudder away !

Shot and shell from the fleet at anchor,
    Shot and shell from shore and shore :
Torpedoes and mines upheaving,
    A deafening, hellish roar :

A storm of iron hail shrieking,
    Closer the missles fell :
Guns flashed, and the darkness opened
    Like gaps in a roaring hell

Till it seemed as if ship and heroes
    Must be ground beneath the tide.
But the God of War directed,
    And the angry shots flew wide.

SINKING THE MERRIMAC

Fearlessly they worked and quickly,
  Teeth set and brave to a man ;
" On deck ! " rang the clear, sharp order,
  " Cut loose the catamaran ! "

And then the gallant commander,
  When all was well with his crew,
Accomplished in one hurried moment
  What the enemy failed to do.

He touched the explosives, and straightway
  With a hot, spasmodic breath,
The Merrimac heaved in the middle
  And sank to her glorious death.

A cheer went up from the Spaniards,
  And the firing died away ;
And they found eight floating heroes
  On a raft at break of day.

Not a soul was harmed among them,
  For the God of War had planned,
And the Prince of the Spanish navy
  Bore them in safety to land.

Great deeds have been done in battle,
  Of valor there is no lack ;
But none have been greater, braver,
  Than the dash of the Merrimac.

"REMEMBER THE MAINE."

When wavering o'er your nation's pride,
When moments of peace steal in ;
When fear and courage run side by side
At the thought of battle's din,
Remember the Maine!

When reading sweet messages of peace,
When slumber falleth at night :
When doubt and fears by day increase,
When asking your God for light,
Remember the Maine!

When sighting across a bar of steel
At devils who pose as men,
List to our dead sailors' mute appeal,
Remember, O comrades, then,
Remember the Maine!

THE GUNGAWAMP WAR PROPHET.

He sot eroun the village store all threw the recent
war,
Explainin tew the other chaps what this an that wuz
for;
An ev'ry time a move wuz made upon the lan or sea,
Resultin in our victory, "I tol yew so," said he.
Ez early ez the Maine went down, he knew 'twuz
goin tur be;
"I tol yew they would do it, boys, I tol yew so,"
said he.
An wen George Dewey sunk the fleet uv Adm'ral
Montejo,
"I tol yew he could do it, boys, yew know I tol
yew so."

An wen Cevera's loafin place wuz foun with skill
an care,
Jim Martin tol us ev'ry one he knowed thet he wuz
there;
An wen the Merrimac wuz sunk beneath the rest-
less tide,
Jim Martin smoked his pipe an lowed 'twuz what he
proffersied.
Cevera's dash, an Sampson's chase, an Santiago's
fall,
An Miles's gran reception, an the welcome protocol,

Wuz all foreseen by Jim, altho he kep the facts away,
Until he'd read the papers frum the city ev'ry day.
An Gungawamp no prophet hed one haf ez great ez
    Jim,
Who lowed the board uv strategy should be uv souls
    like him ;
He knew the ropes frum stem tur stern, an ev'ry day
    would pose
In Jones's store an emfersize his mighty "tol yew
    sos,"
But while the war wuz goin on Jim's knowledge took
    a slump,
On matters uv importance takin place in Gungawamp;
An wen wuz twins at Hiram Lord's, Jim wuz a sight
    tur see ;
An ev'ry one haw-hawed an says, "we tol' yew
    so," says we.

A LATE VOLUNTEER.

I'm going to volunteer, that's all,
    I am.
'Tis not my noble country's call,
    Not Sam.

Poor Will went to the Philipines,
    And fell;
A vacancy at home that means—
    Ah, well!

He left a maiden fair—poor Will -
    Sweet Grace;
I'm going to volunteer to fill
    Will's place!

VOLUNTEER JIM.

Yew see thet field uv wavin corn, an thet big patch
    uv wheat?
Yew see them orchards hengin full uv fruit both ripe
    an sweet?
Yew see my garden loaded down with squashes, peas
    an beans,
An see thet henyard full uv fowls, with eggs behin
    the scenes?
Yew see a hundred head uv stock, them pigs now fat
    tur kill,
An see five hundred fatted sheep off grazin on the
    hill?
Yew see our pantry brimmin o'er with goodies sweet
    an rare,
An signs uv farm prosperity, an plenty everywhere?
Ah, yes, it's ben a wondrous year, the like we never
    knew,
No sech a yieldin up uv crops since back in eighty-
    two.

An wen I think uv this here stuff, an Jim way off
    down there,
It makes me shet my fist down hard an curse out my
    dispair.
I tell yew sir, they's murder there, it makes my
    anger boil,

Tur think they starved my only boy off there on Cuban
    soil !
They starved him, sir at San Juan, long sence the
    battle's cheer,
An I grow sick tur think uv it, while we hed plenty
    here.
A-plenty here at home, sir, an Jim a-starvin there ;
It makes me shet my fist down hard, an curse out my
    dispair.
Someone's tur blame fur thet black crime, an may the
    good Lord lead
Him frum the wrath uv my right arm which burns
    tur squar thet deed !

Jim left the farm an jined the ranks a brave young
    volunteer ;
Wuz in the charge at San Juan, an wuzz't't hurt I
    hear,
But sickness took him down, an then he lay without
    no care.
An couldn't eat his rations an he died a-wantin there.
It's hard tur die in sech a way—it's easy in a fight.
Wen one is full uv loyalty, an wen his cause is
    right—
But, sir, they's vengeance in my heart—it drives me
    tur dispair.
Tur think we hed a-plenty here, an Jim a-starvin
    there !

SOME HARD QUESTIONS.

The feller on my knee,
   Says he,
" What is the war about ?
What makes they shoot each other down,
An' blow up ships an' all get drown' ?
  Why can't they do without ? "
   Says he
   To me.

The feller on my knee,
   Says he.
" An' has you got to go ?
An' is you goin' to leave mamma
An' me, an' march away so far ?
  You'll sorry be, I know,"
   Says he
   To me.

The feller on my knee,
   Says he,
" Will you come back again ? "
I put him down, I could not speak,
A tear fell on his upturned cheek—
  " I hate old cruel Spain,"
   Says he
   To me.

KEEP HER STEADY, MR. PILOT.

Let the traitors whine and shiver,
  Let the weaklings hide their heads;
Let the cowards knife the victors,
  If they wish to, in the night:
Let the purple gore of Boston
  Bite and snarl like quadrupeds,
We are with you, Bill M'Kinley,
  For we know that you are right.

Let them turn against the saviour
  Of the country's policy,
Whom they worshipped like a Master
  Only back in Ninety Six;
Whom they raised to save the nation
  From a dire calamity—
We are with you, Bill M'Kinley,
  Both in war and politics.

O this flimsy human nature
  When it goes against the grain;
O the blindness of a mortal
  When he will not see the light:
Keep her steady, Mr. Pilot,
  There is sunshine thro' the rain,
We are with you, Bill M'Kinley,
  For we know that you are right.

THE BATTLESHIP OREGON.

Sing ho ! a song for the Oregon,
 The warrior of the deep ;
The great sea-hound who with maddened bound,
 And a growl at every leap,
Bore down on the fleeing enemy,
 With a fire that scorched and tore
Till the Spanish fleet she had rushed to meet
 Was smashed against Cuba's shore.

Sing ho ! a song for the race she ran,
 From the far off Western seas :
With a whitened jaw, and a hungry paw,
 And a curse flung to the breeze.
Boast ye of the fourteen thousand miles,
 To avenge her sister ship !
Boast ye of the shot which thundered hot
 From her round and blood-red lip.

Sing ho ! a song for the cruise she made
 From the West to Manila Bay ;
With never a halt from flaw or fault,
 And ready to join the fray.
Then three times three for the Oregon,
 The mightiest dog of war !
The hope and more of the lives ashore,
 The pride of the Yankee tar.

•

Books in Preparation

By the Same Author.

MILL BALLADS

Poems of Factory Life.

PAPER, 25 CENTS.

...These poems are descriptive of New England factory and village life, dating from the present back to sixty years ago, when the little mill under the hill was peopled with laughing country girls, and when the hours of labor were from daylight till dark the year round. New England factory life is one vast field of romance and poetry.

SADE THE CRIMSON GIRL

A Romance of Harvard Square.

A NOVEL. PAPER, 25 CENTS.

...This story faithfully pictures a side of college life never before written for public print. The adventures of students, mill girls and variety actresses should form chapters of interesting and spicy reading.